The Reader's Digestive
by William Jackson

An Illustrated Walk Through the World of the Biscuit

The Reader's Digestive
by William Jackson

Illustrated by Mr Gresty
© 🌰 Mr Gresty 2012

First Edition: November 2012

The Introduction

Good afternoon.

I have been enchanted by biscuits for as long as I can remember, which is longer than it should be. Some of my fondest childhood memories are hazy recollections of receiving my daily ration of two biscuits. These after-school victuals, stored in the sacred barrel, would be the highlight of any a youthful day. Never fully knowing the contents of the biscuit tin always added to the mystique of this treasure trove. On discovering one of the more upmarket varieties accommodated within, I would rejoice, and pray for the day I was in charge of purchasing my own groceries. That day has arrived.

It is this obsession, which has inspired me to attempt to bring to life some of the more abstract and intangible qualities of the humble biscuit.

I have made a selection of twenty-five specimens for your perusal. There are far too many citizens and denizens of Planet Biscuit to include purposefully, as such I have whittled away any superfluous inclusions. Various mongrels and unsolicited amalgams that sit atop the shelf of your local convenience store hold no place in the classic canon of the biscuit. My choices are what I consider to be the classics and the staples with a few latter-day additions I feel are worthy of mention.

These choices might well be something with which you strongly disagree, and that is indeed the essence of this book - to provoke debate. That I deem a Custard Cream biscuit worthy of approbation may be an insult to you. That there are certain incarnations of biscuit which I believe illustrate all that is wrong with humanity, may be contrary to your views.

I should point out at this stage that some of the biscuits featured are made by one brand alone, but in most cases it is reasonable to assume they are generic for the purposes of argument.

For a more fact or scientifically-based resource on biscuits, I recommend you conduct your research elsewhere. For a surreal discourse on the meaning of biscuits to me (and ultimately to you), I give you the the Reader's Digestive. Both barrels, as it were.

The Party Ring

4/10

Par-ty! Par-ty!

Most biscuits with a gaping hole in the middle put themselves instantly at a disadvantage. The Party Ring is no exception. It brings to mind an American style doughnut - compressed under intense heat and glazed. More a saccharine-coated ring of ceramic than a biscuit, it shatters rather than crumbles in the mouth. There is the danger of viewing this biscuit through rose-tinted spectacles; fine for the under-7s, but most enjoyed before the parcel has been passed, and the memory fully formed.

The Bourbon Cream

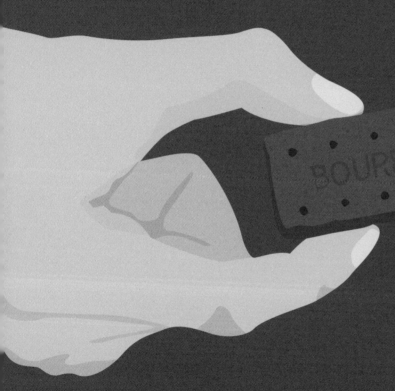

Wonderful Biscuit

The two-bite consumption of the Bourbon is one of life's true pleasures. Biscuits with cream in have to work pretty damn hard to be unpleasant, but the Bourbon refuses to take this for granted. Classic lines have allowed the Bourbon to survive the fads of recent times, and it remains a relevant biscuit today. The only criticism one can level is that it can be improved upon, lest we forget the Penguin bar is essentially a Bourbon cocooned in chocolate. Nonetheless, a cornerstone in my view.

8/10

The Custard Cream

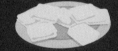

Sweet & Sour?

Caucasian cousin to the Bourbon, the Custard Cream speaks for itself. One of several staple biscuits, it is synonymous with the very word 'biscuit'. As with all the greats, it is a snack in perpetual conflict. The sweet/sour war which has been raging since its inception is what draws one back to the Custard Cream. In my quest for answers, I have demolished packet after packet. This may also be attributable to its perfectly dainty scale. Decorated

Best Consumed
On a full moon

8/10

The Chocolate Chip Cookie

8

Milk

Morning!

A frightfully English take on an American biscuit. The very name is nonsense. That said, as with many things American they do know what they're doing - the blues for example. Being of American lineage, it follows that it's arguably the best breakfast biscuit on the market. The fact that it is not generally suitable for those with a nut allergy does lend it some degree of exclusivity, and the chocolate chip does pose several interesting questions of texture. Certainly not a biscuit to decline, but just lacking an edge.

7/10

The Ginger Nut

Knock Down Ginger!

An unsurprisingly fiery customer. Nevertheless, more-ish beyond many of its competitors. One has to admire the courage of a biscuit which dares be so bold in flavour. It is debatable as to whether any other biscuit could be crunchier yet enjoyed as much as the Ginger Nut is. It is a biscuit of understated quality, distinctive without being ostentatious - it is infectious. Indeed, leave one unchecked in a barrel, and all other varieties inherit more than a hint of its character. Not for the faint-hearted and she does require a fluid foil for maximum enjoyment.

7/10

The Chocolate Digestive

...and another!

Life-affirming biscuit. Justifiably one of the most expensive available, one is always acutely aware that Chocolate Digestives are in the house. Building on the solid foundation of the Digestive, a milk or dark chocolate coating adds that missing yin to an already substantive yang. One can only guess at the circumstances under which chocolate was added. Perhaps a happy accident in the factory, though more likely to have come to the designer in a dream. Words do not do this biscuit justice.

10/10

The Chocolate Shortcake

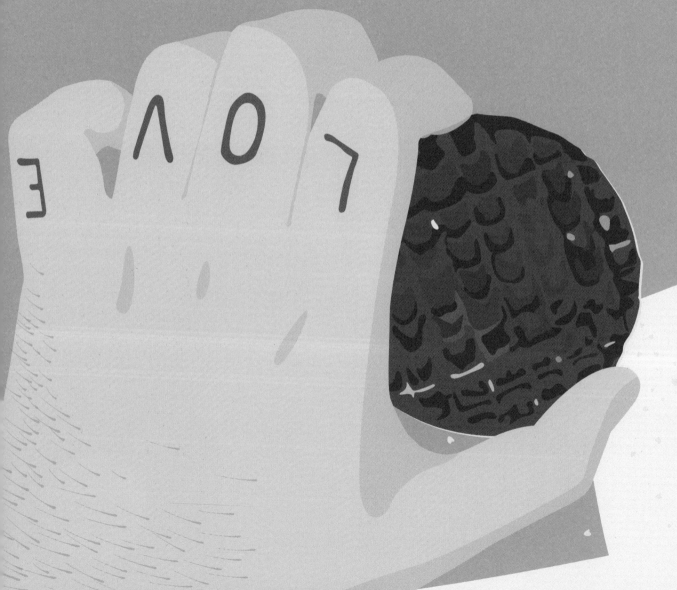

9/10

Good Grief!

If the Chocolate Digestive is the Beatles of the biscuit world, then this is the Stones. A recent introduction into what is widely considered a saturated market, this beast shows there is still room for challengers. As with a sprinter attempting to shave hundredths of a second off the world record, the Chocolate Shortcake has snuck in to give its chief rival (the Chocolate Digestive) a real run for its money. Wind assisted or no, a chocolate-hooded biscuit of this calibre is destined to become a household name.

The Coconut Ring

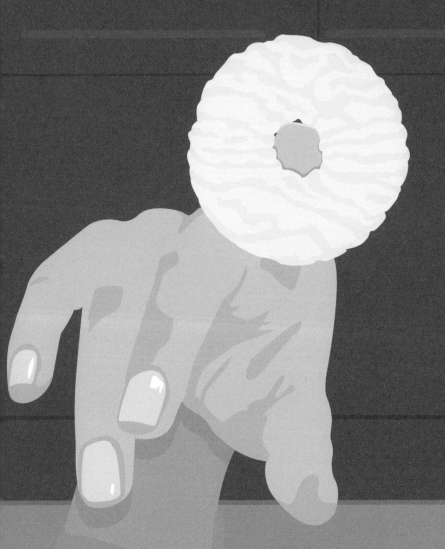

Put another ring on!

Amazingly, the Coconut Ring defies physics by actually increasing its biscuit mass due to the bullet hole that goes right through it. One can only assume that when the owner of the factory was shown the prototype, a sudden spark of inspiration caused him to whip out his pistol and blow the excess away. It somehow has almost lunar qualities, or more accurately could be one of Saturn's rings. I find myself constantly irked at the sheer public ignorance toward coconut as a biscuit flavour. It is surely to earn accolades in years to come.

Best Consumed
Near the oven

7/10

The Rich Tea

ROUND

RICH TEA

BISCUITS

Humble

Be it finger or disc, the Rich Tea is a reliable friend. Throwaway is the wrong word, but one does almost dispose of rather than savour this example. Let us first extol the virtues of the Rich Tea before deriding its mediocrity. The instructional value of the suggested accompanying beverage is to be applauded. It may not be as glamorous as an erudite wheel of brie proposing that we select an '86 Sauvignon, but it is no-nonsense and indeed correct in hinting at the fact its inherent blandness can be redressed with a cup of tea. Humble.

5/10

The Hobnob

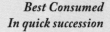
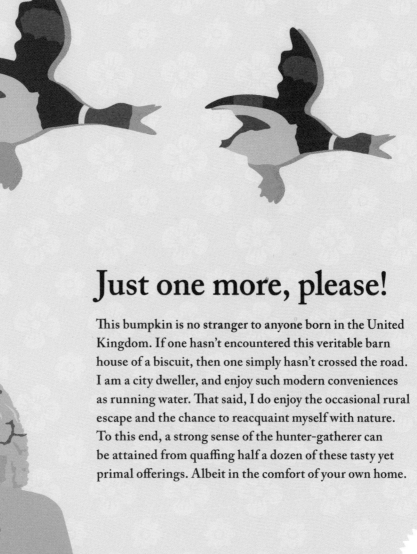

Just one more, please!

This bumpkin is no stranger to anyone born in the United Kingdom. If one hasn't encountered this veritable barn house of a biscuit, then one simply hasn't crossed the road. I am a city dweller, and enjoy such modern conveniences as running water. That said, I do enjoy the occasional rural escape and the chance to reacquaint myself with nature. To this end, a strong sense of the hunter-gatherer can be attained from quaffing half a dozen of these tasty yet primal offerings. Albeit in the comfort of your own home.

7/10

The Malted Milk

No ball games

6/10

Sir 4 Miss!

The Sacred Cow livery gives this biscuit an air of authority. I have always approached the Malted Milk with some trepidation; as though walking down the corridor to see the headmaster when you suspect he knows you did it. One needn't be so worried though, it's more of a request to do some public reading than a berating for attempting stand-up comedy in geography. One feels a sort of nervous pride with this biscuit in hand, always thinking a good old Digestive would be preferable.

The Fruit Shortcake

8/10

...are we there yet?

Not the first deceptively good biscuit ever made, but one of the best. Possibly the greatest, and most under-employed qualities biscuitkind possesses is to deceive. One occasionally feels somewhat ambivalent when offered certain snack discs, as with this candidate. The error of one's ways is rapidly acknowledged however, as the duel threat of crunch and chew is deployed. Maybe the grains of sugar (the size of dice) used as a garnish skew judgment due to the immense rush, but I give it the benefit of the doubt.

The Pink Wafer

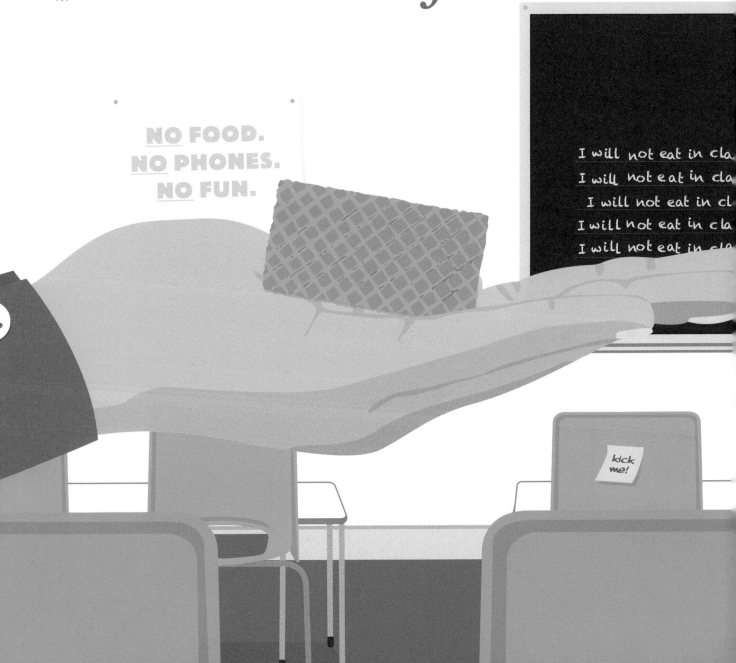

I will not eat in class I will not eat in class
I will not eat in class I will not e...
will not eat in class I will not e...
I will not eat in class I will not ea...
I will not eat in class I will not ea...
I will not eat in class I will not e...

Sorry, Sir!

Made from reclaimed primary school ceiling tiles, the Pink Wafer is quite the dandy. Unashamedly garish and somewhat risqué, it's a hit with grandma. I've never quite understood why so many grandmothers embrace this biscuit, and indeed the kind of innuendo and seedy glamour that go with it. Perhaps the instant association with the flamingo alludes to an exotic quality, but it's more Butlins than Botswana. Ingesting one of these is akin to watching a musical on television under duress.

4/10

The Garibaldi

No.14

Squash it!

Despite being raised in a household which referred to
the Garibaldi as the "squashed-fly biscuit", it holds a
place in my biscuit tin. Arguably more rustic than a
Hobnob, the crudeness of its construction is plainly
evident. The Garibaldi comes in sheets, only scored
by the machinery from which it was hewn. One
imagines hectares of the stuff being slowly chopped in
industrial workhouses, the foreman praying for a good
harvest. Perhaps a slightly more hands-on approach to
manufacture would improve what is a good biscuit.

7/10

No.*15*

The Lincoln Shortcake

6/10

Heavenly?

One of the most stylish on the market, in visual terms. The Modernist façia is almost foreboding, like a manhole cover. The Lincoln is manufactured on a metalworking lathe - aluminium with a citrus hint. And therein lies the fundamental problem with this customer - it lacks soul. Like the Tin Man wearing a fine cologne, the Lincoln is not unpleasant to be around but not the first person to invite to the party. It is perhaps the biscuit Bauhaus never designed, or something Le Corbusier might have sketched (on the back of a packet of Nice).

The Jam Ring

Jammy Lad!

Another juvenile biscuit, cut from a similar cloth to the Party Ring. There is however, more than nostalgic pleasure to be derived from eating these treats. They are an affordable and easy way to emulate a high tea, and it is not too great a stretch of the imagination to picture them on the shelves of Fortnum & Mason. Some considerable re-design would be required to the packaging if these were to pass muster for His or Her Majesty however. A decent bloke, is this biscuit, though perhaps not one with whom to consort after dinner.

The Digestive

Back to Basics!

A more archetypal biscuit there has surely never been. Quintessentially British, they will be rationed during the next World War (and a treat they will be). Only just sweet enough to be classed a biscuit, indeed, a fine accompaniment to cheese. The sweet-meal option has to be the superior of the two available - the wholemeal being the biscuit choice of a person who feels remorse for even entering the biscuit aisle of their local grocer. The perfect introduction for anyone living yet to try a biscuit - basic but virtuous.

Best Consume
In a field

6/10

No. 18

The Lemon Puff

3/10

…like a lemon?

Bit of a damp squib really. Far too weak to call itself a biscuit with any real conviction, the Lemon Puff is more a stale biscuit for cheese than fresh biscuit for pleasure. Lemon and biscuit do not tend to make good bedfellows. The carbon footprint created by this waste of a manufacturing process is inexcusable. That fact that environmental groups are yet to intervene is puzzling given the current climate. A Lemon Puff in the hand is not worth two in the bush.

i'll do anything for food, but i wont do that!

KEEP OFF THE ASS

Nice to see you, to see you…

Something of a continental biscuit, the Nice. It sounds French, and does possess a certain arrogance. Waif-like and low on constituent elements, one of the few discernible characteristics is the word NICE etched into the thing. Granted, it is nice, but to spell it out is unnecessary; a more English biscuit such as the Rich Tea sees no reason to brand itself with the word REASONABLE. The Nice is at its best in the afternoon with tea (and a good selection of doilies), preferably after waking from a well-earned nap.

6/10

No.20

The Chocolate Hobnob

ARCADE

9/10

CHOCOLATE Hobnobs

High Score!

This barnstormer is not to be trifled with. Part feral, part gentry, the Chocolate Hobnob is a real loose cannon. As with several other biscuits, the combination of dichotomous elements works splendidly. In this case it is as though some wandering genius decided to guild the grass, rather than the lily. This inspired restraint has produced a real leader of the pack. If ever I were to bear the responsibility of entering biscuits for international competition, I would send this candidate to Zurich (for example) expecting medals.

The Fig Roll

Roll with it!

This borderline biscuit says something about
our ancestors. A relic of a biscuit, I can only
guess it must have been a delicacy of the
Roman and Ottoman Empires. As far as what
the Romans have done for us goes, the Fig Roll
ranks alongside drainage systems - and goes
some way towards atoning for Opera. Not all
the way however. It is not alone in pushing
the bounds of what a biscuit is, but despite my
liberal disposition I struggle to trust it fully.
After all, if all 'biscuits' hardened with age,
then they would essentially hold the key to
eternal life.

8/10

The Shortbread Finger

Pull my wee-finger!

This Highlander is a remnant of the bloody history shared by England and Scotland. It is a biscuit at war, ruthlessly annihilating its rivals. It's a brut: thick, tough, and rough around the edges. Yet its subtle flavour offers us a paradox. It's as though she feels she has to go around savaging everyone in order to convince them of how nice she is. This is of course unnecessary, but try to reason with a biscuit of this stature and you're asking for trouble with a capital T. Definitely on the podium in anyone's biscuit Olympics - you're a fool if you can't see that.

10/10

The Ginger / Golden Crunch

◀ EXIT

◀ EXIT

Best Consumed
Any empty car park

Get 1 Free!

You'll have probably noticed by now that this entry involves not one, but two biscuits. The likeness of these biscuit siblings is such that they ought to be mentioned in the same breath. Edible yo-yos as these particular Crunches are, they owe a debt to the Custard Cream. Whilst the RRP suggests there is a gulf in quality, this is not evident in real terms. A cream-filled biscuit will always engender a certain degree of excitement upon gazing into the biscuit tin, and these chaps go some way toward rewarding that sense. Charlatan is too harsh a word, perhaps a sheep in wolf's clothing is a fair assessment.

8/10

The Crinkle

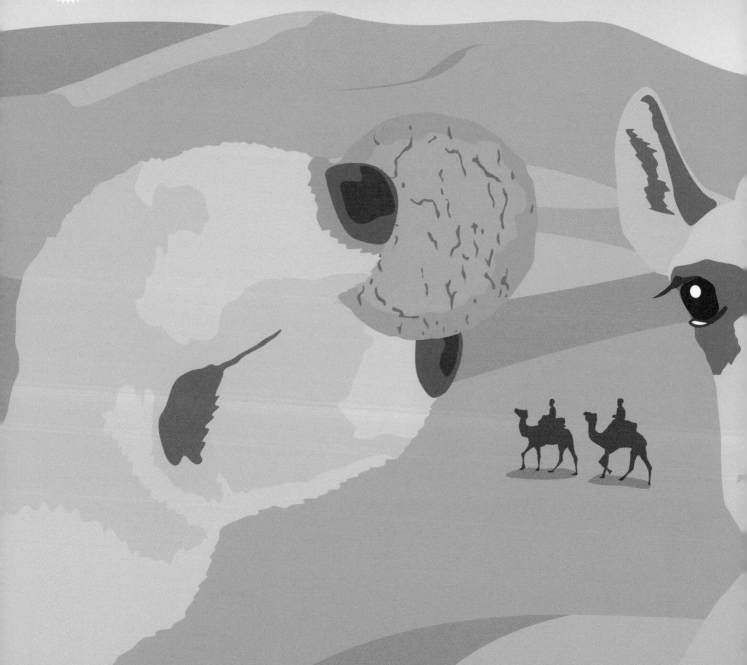

Just a Mirage

A brand-specific product, this biscuit is worthy of mention. Essentially the result of ramming a block of butter through a beehive (though I am yet to conduct the experiment myself), this is a rich character. The appearance is analogous to that of a desert - parched and cracked. This is the only real fault I can find with it. A great biscuit can be enjoyed in the absence of any fluid, and would indeed make for a welcome oasis. The Crinkle falls narrowly short of its rivals in this context, but in the right setting can be eaten well into double figures.

8/10

The Jaffa Cake

No.25

9/10

Cake?

According to V.A.T. classification, the Jaffa Cake is technically a cake. Plus, it's called a Jaffa *Cake*. That said, like an adopted sibling one grows to like, it is a welcome addition to the (biscuit) family. There is something of the breakfast about her, marmalade being the blood coursing through atriums of chocolate and sponge. This slightly bland sponge is the chief shortcoming of an excellent if dubious resident of the biscuit shelf. The substitution of a biscuit base to the Jaffa is something I dream of one day tasting.

The Results

4/10

No. 1
The Party Ring

8/10

No. 2
The Bourbon Cream

8/10

No. 3
The Custard Cream

7/10

No. 4
The Chocolate Chip Cookie

7/10

No. 5
The Ginger Nut

10/10

No. 6
The Chocolate Digestive

9/10

No. 7
The Chocolate Shortcake

7/10

No. 8
The Coconut Ring

5/10

No. 9
The Rich Tea

7/10

No. 10
The Hobnob

6/10

No. 11
The Malted Milk

8/10

No. 12
The Fruit Shortcake

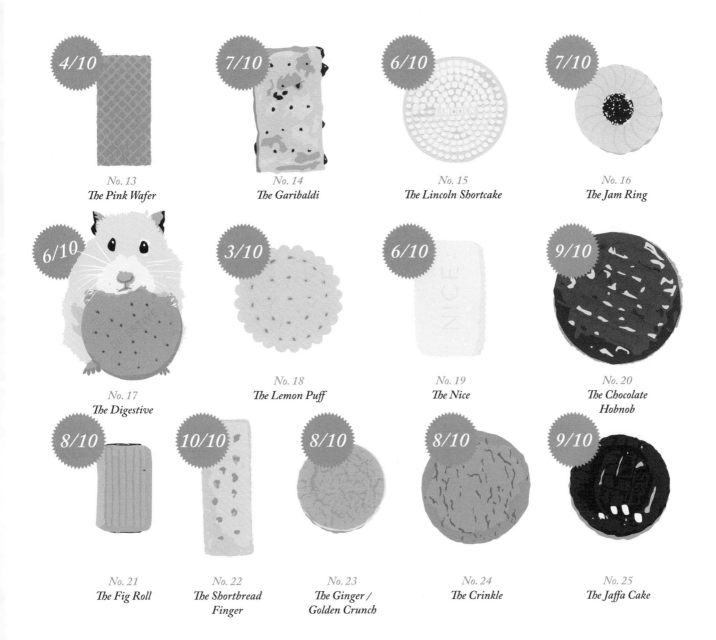

Crumbs! It's just my opinion!
What do you think?

4/10

No. 13
The Pink Wafer

7/10

No. 14
The Garibaldi

6/10

No. 15
The Lincoln Shortcake

7/10

No. 16
The Jam Ring

6/10

No. 17
The Digestive

3/10

No. 18
The Lemon Puff

6/10

No. 19
The Nice

9/10

No. 20
*The Chocolate
Hobnob*

8/10

No. 21
The Fig Roll

10/10

No. 22
*The Shortbread
Finger*

8/10

No. 23
*The Ginger /
Golden Crunch*

8/10

No. 24
The Crinkle

9/10

No. 25
The Jaffa Cake

The Conclusion

So there you have it. I do hope that you are not overly upset with any of my opinions. I am certain that you will disagree vehemently with many of my assertions. That's fine. You are entitled to do so. You may even feel the desire to write your own ripostes. I would welcome any such correspondance. This would make the Reader's Digestive a success.

Should that prove to be the case, I will feel justified in undertaking the writing of a sequel. My ambition is to travel the great biscuit nations of Europe. France, Italy, and in particular, Holland are just some of the countries I intend to visit with the sole aim of biscuit tourism. I have always felt that one can learn more from the cuisine of a people than from say, the architecture. The Palladian buildings of Rome may reveal how the Italians used to live, but pale in comparison to what we can learn from their contemporary biscuits.

We all know that the French are great producers of wine, but how much do we know about really know about their bis coctus? Very little I suspect. I hope this volume reveals elements of English sensibility, of the restraint and dignity embodied in so many of our biscuits. I would hypothesise that my perception of the people of France as more indulgent could be proven by the butter content of their sweet snacks. With any luck, I'll amass the necessary funds to conduct my not-entirely-scientific research this decade.

This is all pie in the sky at present though, it would be more prudent to focus on biscuits in the cupboard for the immediate future. With that in mind, I will embark on the short trip to my local grocer's, and purchase a packet of twice-cooked treats. Perhaps some Chocolate Digestives, for today is a good day.